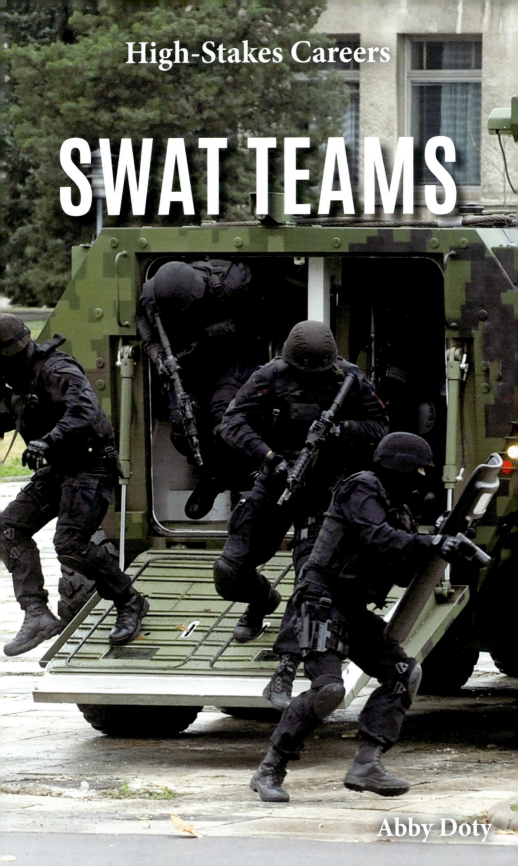

High-Stakes Careers

SWAT TEAMS

Abby Doty

WWW.APEXEDITIONS.COM

Copyright © 2026 by Apex Editions, Mendota Heights, MN 55120. All rights reserved. No part of this book may be reproduced or utilized in any form or by any means without written permission from the publisher.

Apex is distributed by North Star Editions:
sales@northstareditions.com | 888-417-0195

Produced for Apex by Red Line Editorial.

Photographs ©: Shutterstock Images, cover, 1, 4–5, 8–9, 10–11, 12–13, 14–15, 16–17, 18–19, 20–21, 24–25, 26–27, 29, 40–41, 49, 50–51, 52–53, 54–55, 56–57, 58; Gary McCullough/AP Images, 6–7; iStockphoto, 22–23, 32–33, 34–35, 36–37, 38–39; Brendan Smialowski/AFP/Getty Images, 30–31; Kevork Djansezian/Getty Images News/Getty Images, 42–43; Andres Morales/The Lima News/AP Images, 44–45; Mark DuFrene/Contra Costa Times/ZUMA Press/Alamy, 46–47

Library of Congress Control Number: 2025930925

ISBN
979-8-89250-674-8 (hardcover)
979-8-89250-708-0 (ebook pdf)
979-8-89250-692-2 (hosted ebook)

Printed in the United States of America
Mankato, MN
082025

NOTE TO PARENTS AND EDUCATORS

Apex books are designed to build literacy skills in striving readers. Exciting, high-interest content attracts and holds readers' attention. The text is carefully leveled to allow students to achieve success quickly.

TABLE OF CONTENTS

Chapter 1
TO THE RESCUE 4

Chapter 2
WHAT ARE SWAT TEAMS? 8

Chapter 3
WHAT SWAT TEAMS DO 18

Story Spotlight
FREEING HOSTAGES 28

Chapter 4
MANY ROLES 30

Chapter 5
RISKS 40

Story Spotlight
HURT ON THE JOB 48

Chapter 6
TYPES OF TRAINING 50

SKILLS CHECKLIST • 59
COMPREHENSION QUESTIONS • 60
GLOSSARY • 62
TO LEARN MORE • 63
ABOUT THE AUTHOR • 63
INDEX • 64

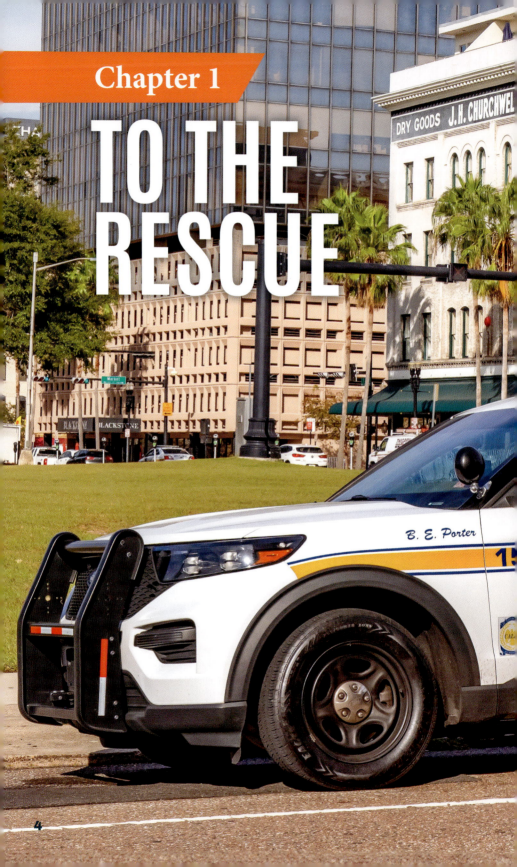

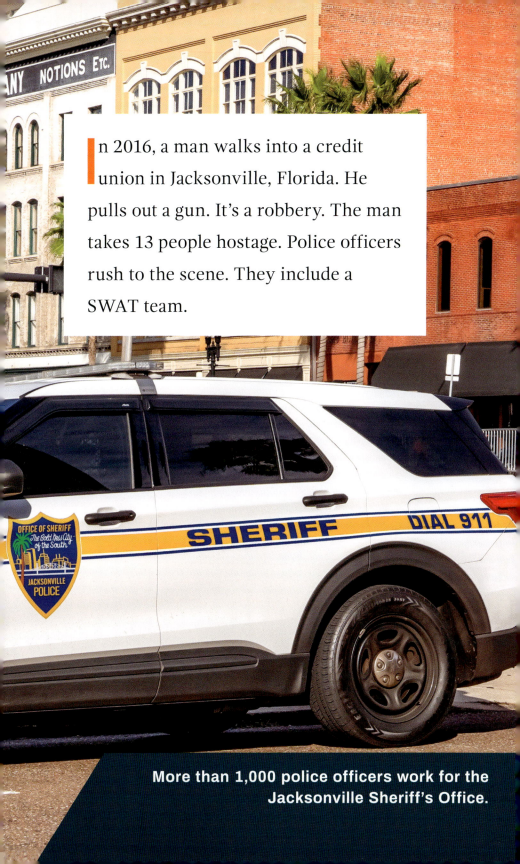

In 2016, a man walks into a credit union in Jacksonville, Florida. He pulls out a gun. It's a robbery. The man takes 13 people hostage. Police officers rush to the scene. They include a SWAT team.

More than 1,000 police officers work for the Jacksonville Sheriff's Office.

The SWAT team tries talking with the man. He agrees to let a few hostages go. But he says he will hurt the others. He points his gun at them.

Two credit union workers try sneaking out the front. That distracts the hostage taker. SWAT officers swarm the credit union. They tell the man to get down. He finally gives up, and they arrest him.

Police gathered outside the credit union to help free the hostages.

CAUGHT

The robber kept people trapped in the credit union for about two hours. Someone walking by saw and called 911. All the hostages got out safely. And the robber was sentenced to 15 years in prison.

Chapter 2

WHAT ARE SWAT TEAMS?

SWAT stands for "Special Weapons and Tactics." SWAT teams are part of US police forces. They respond to high-risk situations. So, their members have extra weapons and training.

LOS ANGELES POLICE

S.W.A.T.

The Los Angeles Police Department had the first SWAT team ever. It formed in 1967.

In 1966, a man killed 14 people by shooting from the University of Texas's clock tower.

The first SWAT teams formed in the late 1960s. The 1960s were a time of unrest. Riots and mass shootings took place. Many people got hurt. Police departments wanted to keep order. So, they formed teams of officers who focused on responding to threats.

TEXAS TOWER SHOOTING

In 1966, a man climbed the clock tower at the University of Texas at Austin. He shot many people. Police officers didn't know what to do. So, they took a long time to stop him. Afterward, many police departments made plans for dealing with this type of event. They also added more training for officers.

Full-time SWAT officers are on call every day of the week. They can get called to work at any time of day or night.

Today, many city police departments have SWAT teams. Other teams work for a county or state. They help police throughout this area. The US government has its own SWAT team, too. It responds to major emergencies. For example, a person might try to hurt the president. Or someone might capture many hostages.

DOUBLE DUTY

At some police departments, officers serve on SWAT teams full-time. But it's more often a part-time position. The rest of the time, officers do other police work. For example, they may go on patrol.

13

Armored trucks have thick sides and strong windows that can block bullets.

SWAT teams rush to the scenes of crimes or crises. They may help catch suspects. Or they may save people from danger. Teams usually ride in armored trucks. They bring weapons and body armor.

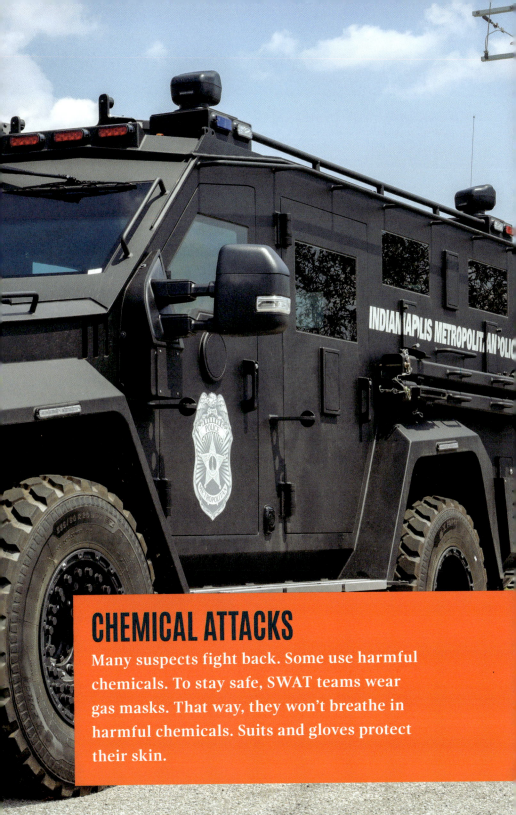

CHEMICAL ATTACKS

Many suspects fight back. Some use harmful chemicals. To stay safe, SWAT teams wear gas masks. That way, they won't breathe in harmful chemicals. Suits and gloves protect their skin.

SWAT teams try to end threats peacefully. Teams may talk with suspects. They try to get them to give up. Some suspects do. Other times, SWAT teams must catch them. To do this, teams may break into buildings. Or they may sneak in carefully. Teams may also use flash-bangs. These small bombs make loud noises and bright flashes. Teams throw them to stun suspects. Then teams can rush in and take the suspects down.

If these ways don't work, teams may use more force. But in most cases, they don't hurt suspects.

SWAT teams may use ropes to climb up or down the sides of buildings.

17

Chapter 3

WHAT SWAT TEAMS DO

SWAT teams are trained to handle a variety of dangerous situations. Many involve violent crimes. Teams may help catch armed robbers. Or they may work to stop active shooters.

SWAT teams may use shields for protection.

SWAT officers may stand guard at big events or famous places.

20

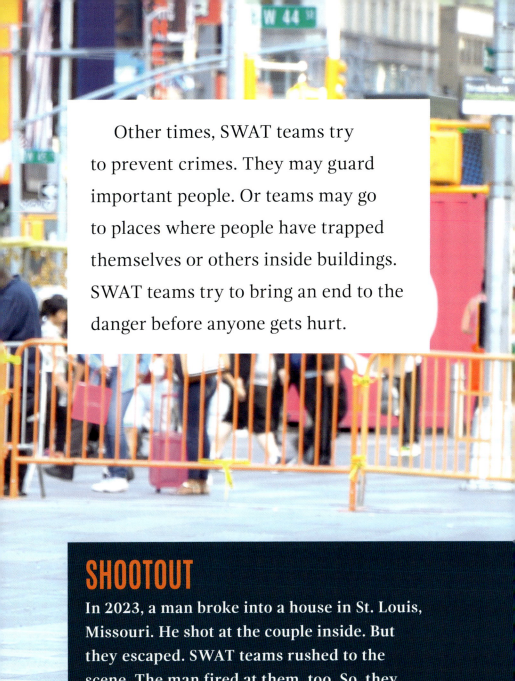

Other times, SWAT teams try to prevent crimes. They may guard important people. Or teams may go to places where people have trapped themselves or others inside buildings. SWAT teams try to bring an end to the danger before anyone gets hurt.

SHOOTOUT

In 2023, a man broke into a house in St. Louis, Missouri. He shot at the couple inside. But they escaped. SWAT teams rushed to the scene. The man fired at them, too. So, they shot back and hit him. They brought him to the hospital. No one else got hurt.

SWAT teams also help with hostage situations. SWAT teams talk with hostage takers. Teams try to learn what people are planning. And they try to convince people to let the hostages go. If talking doesn't work, team members may sneak in and attack.

SWAT teams may attack at night to surprise suspects.

SWAT teams do raids as well. In a raid, a team bursts into a home or building. They may arrest a suspect. Or they may look for evidence of crime. For example, they may search for illegal drugs.

To do a raid, a team must get a search warrant. This gives them permission to enter.

NO-KNOCK WARRANTS

For some warrants, police must give warnings before going inside. "No-knock warrants" let teams enter by surprise. Suspects don't have time to hide or get rid of things. But sudden searches are dangerous. Suspects may think robbers are breaking in. So, they may attack.

During raids, SWAT teams often search for weapons, drugs, or stolen items.

25

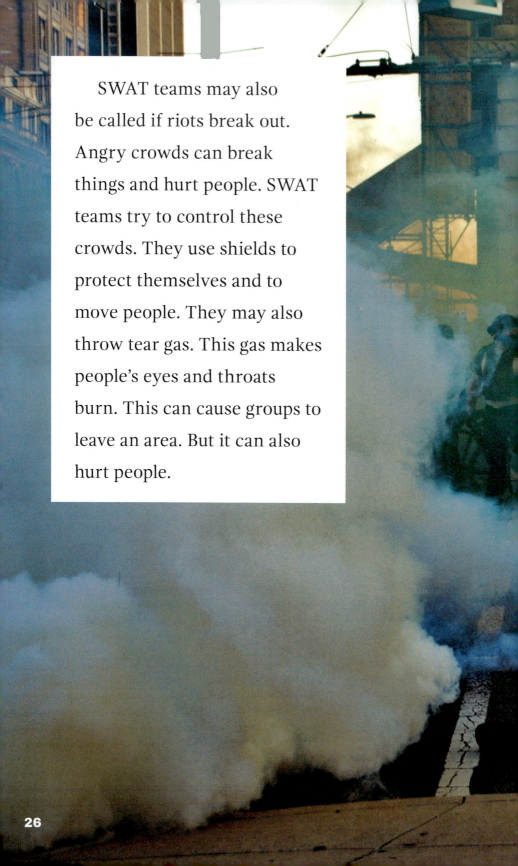

SWAT teams may also be called if riots break out. Angry crowds can break things and hurt people. SWAT teams try to control these crowds. They use shields to protect themselves and to move people. They may also throw tear gas. This gas makes people's eyes and throats burn. This can cause groups to leave an area. But it can also hurt people.

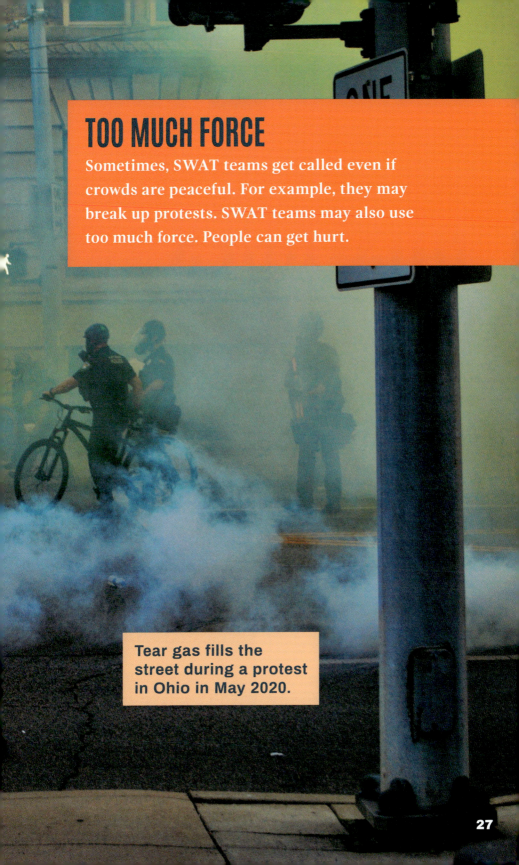

TOO MUCH FORCE

Sometimes, SWAT teams get called even if crowds are peaceful. For example, they may break up protests. SWAT teams may also use too much force. People can get hurt.

Tear gas fills the street during a protest in Ohio in May 2020.

27

Story Spotlight

FREEING HOSTAGES

In 2024, a man in Pennsylvania trapped his wife and kids in an apartment. He wouldn't let them leave. He said he would hurt them. The wife escaped. But the man still held the children hostage.

A SWAT team came to help. They tried talking with the man for two hours. He wouldn't leave. So, they threw flash-bangs inside the building. The man finally came out. SWAT officers saved the children and arrested the man.

Flash-bangs make it hard for people to see or hear for several seconds.

Chapter 4

MANY ROLES

The size of a SWAT team can vary. Some teams have fewer than 10 people. Others have dozens of members. Each team has a commander. This person leads the team.

Some SWAT teams are part of the FBI. These teams can have more than 40 members.

Other team members have different roles. Breachers are one example. They help teams get into buildings where people are trapped or hiding. Breachers help choose where the team enters. They may find ways to get through doors or windows. Or they may use explosives to blast their way in.

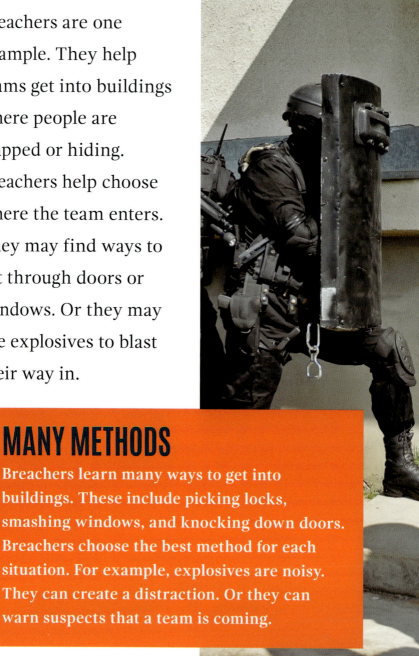

MANY METHODS

Breachers learn many ways to get into buildings. These include picking locks, smashing windows, and knocking down doors. Breachers choose the best method for each situation. For example, explosives are noisy. They can create a distraction. Or they can warn suspects that a team is coming.

SWAT teams may use rams or hammers to break down doors.

A sniper is another role. Snipers usually sit in high places, such as on top of buildings. They watch situations from above. They can tell their team members where suspects are. Snipers look out for danger. If needed, they can shoot. They can hit targets from far away.

EYES IN THE SKY

Snipers prepare for many tricky shots. Targets may be more than 50 yards (46 m) away. And they're often in dark places. Snipers must aim carefully. They don't want to hit hostages or other SWAT members.

Snipers often use powerful rifles.

Crisis negotiators often speak to suspects on the phone. That helps the negotiators stay out of danger.

Many SWAT teams have crisis negotiators. These members speak with suspects. They try to get suspects to give up peacefully. They may ask people to leave a building or let hostages go.

Negotiators try to keep suspects from hurting themselves or others. In most cases, suspects agree to surrender. But if they don't, SWAT teams may use force.

37

Some team members are investigators. They gather information about suspects. They try to learn what people have done and what they plan to do. They also try to learn why. Investigators share what they learn with their team. This helps the team make better plans.

MEDICS

In a crisis, many people can get hurt. So, SWAT teams have medics. They provide medical care right at the scene. They also help people get to hospitals.

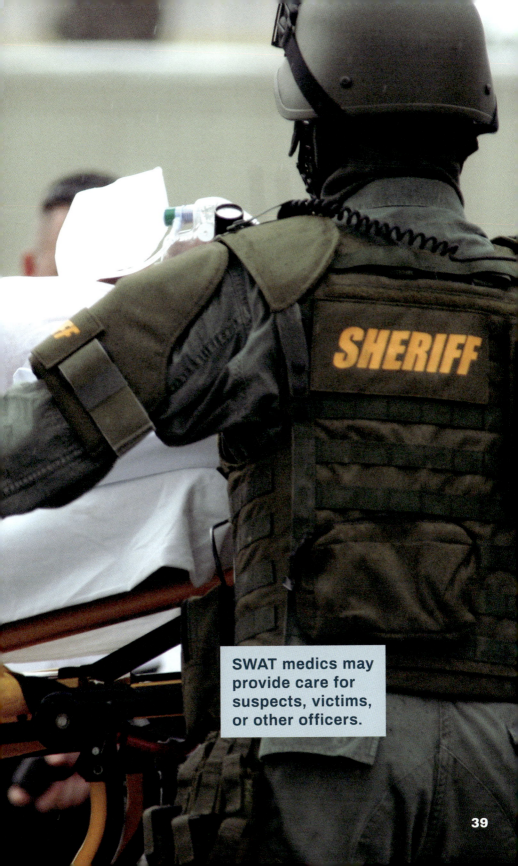

SWAT medics may provide care for suspects, victims, or other officers.

Chapter 5

RISKS

SWAT teams risk their lives when they respond to emergencies. Officers train and plan carefully. But they can still be hurt or killed. Suspects may be armed and desperate.

A California SWAT team responds to reports of a man with a gun in 2021.

A SWAT officer practices climbing down from a helicopter during a drill.

Some challenges are based on location. SWAT teams may use helicopters to reach places quickly. Officers may slide down ropes to reach the ground. Or they may drop onto a building's roof.

Teams may climb up or down the side of a building to get inside. They use ropes for safety. But ropes may break or get tangled. Falls can be deadly.

People protest the death of Tarika Wilson, who was shot when a SWAT team raided her house.

Speed is another challenge. When people are in danger, SWAT teams must act quickly. If they take too long, people can get hurt. But rushing can lead to mistakes. And mistakes can have huge consequences. That's especially true when using force. Innocent people could get hurt or killed.

GONE WRONG

In 2008, SWAT officers threw a flash-bang into a house in Connecticut. They thought men there were using drugs. One officer got stunned by the flash-bang. He thought he'd been shot. So, he fired his gun. He killed one of the men.

Several studies have found that people of color are more likely to face searches or raids than white people.

SWAT teams must decide how much force to use in each situation. This choice can be difficult. Teams try to limit harm. Sometimes, this means taking down a suspect. If they don't, the suspect could hurt people. But teams can sometimes use more force than necessary. For instance, they might think a suspect has a weapon. So, they might shoot. Then, they might learn that the person was unarmed.

FORCE AND BIASES

Biases can shape how much danger people see. For example, SWAT teams are more likely to raid the homes of Black and Latino people. But many times, the teams don't find anything illegal. The people are innocent. Even so, they may get hurt during the raids.

Story Spotlight

HURT ON THE JOB

In 2023, a Texas SWAT team drove after a suspect. They were trying to arrest him. The man shot at them from his car. One bullet hit officer Rhett Shoquist in the eye. He pulled over the car.

Meanwhile, other SWAT cars chased the suspect. They stopped and arrested him. Shoquist went to the hospital. He had many surgeries. He lost his eye. But later, he returned to his SWAT team.

Like people in the military, SWAT teams wear strong goggles that help protect their eyes.

49

Chapter 6

TYPES OF TRAINING

Before joining SWAT teams, most people work as police officers. To become officers, people need high school degrees. Some go to college as well. They often study laws and crimes. Then they complete police training.

On average, police officers train for 21 weeks.

For many missions, SWAT teams must move quickly and quietly through dark, dangerous places.

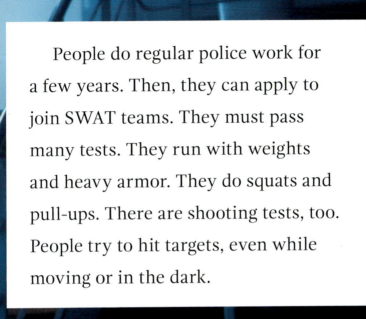

People do regular police work for a few years. Then, they can apply to join SWAT teams. They must pass many tests. They run with weights and heavy armor. They do squats and pull-ups. There are shooting tests, too. People try to hit targets, even while moving or in the dark.

REALISTIC TESTS
Some tests imitate situations that a SWAT team might face. For example, officers may act as suspects. They may pretend to take hostages. Test takers must show what they would do.

SWAT teams practice responding to many types of attacks.

If people pass, they go to SWAT school. There, they learn advanced skills. Students practice driving armored cars. They learn to shoot different kinds of guns. They use grenades and other explosives. Students also practice working in teams. They learn how to help and protect one another during raids or other missions.

TRAINING PLACES

Many missions involve moving quickly and safely through buildings. SWAT teams may use old houses to practice. Or they may make mazes that have rooms, halls, and doors. Team members practice communicating and watching for danger.

55

Snipers often shoot while lying down. This helps their guns stay steady so their aim is as good as possible.

People also train for their specific role on the team. Negotiators learn skills for speaking with people in crisis. Snipers get very good at shooting. And breachers train to work with explosives.

In fact, SWAT teams never stop training. They train and work out together a few days each month. This helps them stay strong and ready to respond.

✓ SKILLS CHECKLIST

- Being tough and strong

- Braving danger to help others

- Moving quickly and quietly

- Thinking calmly and clearly under pressure

- Understanding how to use guns and explosives safely

- Working well with others

COMPREHENSION QUESTIONS

Write your answers on a separate piece of paper.

1. Write a paragraph that explains the main ideas in Chapter 4.

2. If you were part of a SWAT team, which role would you want to have? Why?

3. When did police departments first create SWAT teams?

    A. the late 1960s
    B. the early 2000s
    C. the 2020s

4. What might happen if SWAT teams didn't have snipers?

    A. SWAT teams could work faster.
    B. SWAT teams could find suspects more easily.
    C. SWAT teams could have a harder time seeing suspects.

5. What does **vary** mean in this book?

*The size of a SWAT team can **vary**. Some teams have fewer than 10 people. Others have dozens of members.*

    A. be different
    B. be the exact same
    C. be hard to see

6. What does **information** mean in this book?

*They gather **information** about suspects. They try to learn what people have done and what they plan to do.*

    A. facts about people or things
    B. facts that are not true
    C. ways of moving around

Answer key on page 64.

GLOSSARY

biases
Beliefs that cause people to treat others unequally, often based on what groups others are part of.

communicating
Sending and receiving messages.

credit union
A business that offers banking services.

crises
Times of great danger or serious problems.

explosives
Devices that can blow up, such as bombs.

hostage
Kept as a prisoner until certain demands are met.

innocent
Not involved in any crime or wrongdoing.

protests
Times when people gather to show they disagree with something or call for change.

riots
Times when angry crowds cause damage or problems.

suspects
People the police think may be guilty of a crime.

tactics
Plans that help people win fights or solve problems.

warrant
An order from a judge that allows officers to arrest someone, search an area, or take things as evidence.

TO LEARN MORE

BOOKS

Dolbear, Emily. *Police Officers on the Scene.* The
   Child's World, 2022.
Hamilton, John. *Patrol Cops.* Abdo Publishing,
   2022.
Hamilton, John. *SWAT.* Abdo Publishing, 2022.

ONLINE RESOURCES

Visit **www.apexeditions.com** to find links and
resources related to this title.

ABOUT THE AUTHOR

Abby Doty is a writer, editor, and booklover from
Minnesota.

INDEX

breachers, 32, 57

commander, 30
crimes, 14, 18, 21, 24, 50
crisis negotiators, 37, 57

danger, 14, 18, 21, 24, 34, 45, 47, 55
drugs, 24, 45

emergencies, 13, 40
explosives, 32, 55, 57

flash-bangs, 16, 28, 45

guns, 5–6, 45, 55

helicopters, 43
hostages, 5–7, 13, 22, 28, 35, 37, 53

investigators, 38

missions, 55

police officers, 5, 11, 13, 24, 50

raids, 24, 47, 55
riots, 11, 26
ropes, 43

snipers, 34–35, 57

tear gas, 26
threats, 11, 16
training, 8, 11, 40, 50, 55, 57

warrants, 24
weapons, 8, 14, 46

ANSWER KEY:

1. Answers will vary; 2. Answers will vary; 3. A; 4. C; 5. A; 6. A